# What's the Issue?

# WHAT'S GENDER EQUALITY?

By Katie Kawa

KidHaven PUBLISHING

Published in 2018 by
**KidHaven Publishing, an Imprint of Greenhaven Publishing, LLC**
353 3rd Avenue
Suite 255
New York, NY 10010

Designer: Seth Hughes
Editor: Katie Kawa

Photo credits: Cover (top) Chinnapong/Shutterstock.com; cover (bottom), p. 17 (bottom) © iStockphoto.com/FatCamera; pp. 4, 13 Rawpixel Ltd/iStock/Thinkstock; pp. 5 (top), 7 Digital Vision./Thinkstock; p. 5 (bottom) Rawpixel/iStock/Thinkstock; p. 6 ShutterstockProfessional/ Shutterstock.com; pp. 8–9 © iStockphoto.com/MimaCZ; pp. 10, 18 Epics/Getty Images; p. 11 Photo Researchers/Science Source/Getty Images; p. 12 © iStockphoto.com/monkeybusinessimages; p. 14 leungchopan/Shutterstock.com; p. 15 (top) © iStockphoto.com/Georgijevic; p. 15 (bottom) © iStockphoto.com/baranozdemir; p. 16 Layne Kennedy/Corbis Documentary/Getty Images; p. 17 (top) Klaus Vedfelt/Iconica/Getty Images; p. 19 TONY KARUMBA/AFP/Getty Images; p. 20 ANDREW CABALLERO-REYNOLDS/Staff/AFP/Getty Images; p. 21 (kids) © iStockphoto.com/skynesher; p. 21 (sky) SergeyIT/iStock/Thinkstock.

**Library of Congress Cataloging-in-Publication Data**

Names: Kawa, Katie, author.
Title: What's gender equality? / Katie Kawa.
Description: New York : KidHaven Publishing, [2018] | Series: What's the issue? | Includes bibliographical references and index.
Identifiers: LCCN 2017040249 (print) | LCCN 2017047460 (ebook) | ISBN 9781534524361 (eBook) | ISBN 9781534525030 (pbk. book : alk. paper) | ISBN 9781534524354 (library bound book : alk. paper) | ISBN 9781534525047 (6 pack : alk. paper)
Subjects: LCSH: Sex discrimination–Juvenile literature. | Women's rights–Juvenile literature. | Equality–Juvenile literature. | Feminism–Juvenile literature.
Classification: LCC HQ1237 (ebook) | LCC HQ1237 .K39 2018 (print) | DDC 305.42–dc23
LC record available at https://lccn.loc.gov/2017040249

Printed in the United States of America

CPSIA compliance information: Batch #CW18KL: For further information contact Greenhaven Publishing LLC, New York, New York at 1-844-317-7404.

# CONTENTS

# Fighting for Fairness

Many people around the world fight for equality. This means they want people to be treated the same instead of some groups being treated better than others.

One kind of equality people fight for is gender equality, which is equal **treatment** whether a person is male or female. The fight for gender equality has been going on for a long time, and it's not over yet. Read on to learn how you can help make sure everyone is treated fairly and equally!

4

## Facing the Facts

Gender isn't just based on whether you were born male or female. Gender identity is whether you see yourself as male or female. Gender expression is how you show that to the world.

Do you think boys and girls should have the same opportunities as they grow up? If you do, you believe in gender equality.

# What's Feminism?

When people talk about gender equality, they sometimes use the word "feminism." Different people have different ideas about what that word means. Some people think all feminists believe women are better than men. Other people think feminism is the belief that all men are bad and should have rights taken away from them.

What does feminism actually mean? Its basic **definition** is a belief that women should be treated as men's equals. Feminists aren't just girls and women. Boys and men can be feminists, too!

Feminists aren't all exactly alike. However, they all agree that women and men should be treated as equals.

### Facing the Facts

A 2016 study showed that 53 percent of Americans said they weren't feminists. However, only 11 percent said they believed men and women weren't equal.

# Saying No to Stereotypes

People who fight for gender equality often fight against stereotypes. A stereotype is a belief people have about everyone in a certain group. Stereotypes are often unfair and untrue. They exist because people don't take the time to get to know others who are different.

Stereotypes can be harmful. For example, some people believe the stereotype that girls cry more than boys. This means boys are sometimes picked on for crying, even though it can be healthy to cry. People who believe in gender equality believe both boys and girls should be able to show what they're feeling.

## Facing the Facts

Gender roles are actions and activities that are expected of people because of their gender, such as all girls liking the color pink and all boys liking the color blue. This is true for some boys and girls but not all of them.

# GIRLS and BOYS can

wear pink

wear blue

enjoy cooking

enjoy building things

like math and science

like reading and writing

learn about computers

talk about their feelings

play on a sports team

take dance classes

Gender equality means girls and boys can do things they like to do without worrying about stereotypes or gender roles. Do you like to do any of these things?

# Equal Under the Law

People have fought for gender equality for many years. It took a long time for women in the United States to be granted the right to vote. The U.S. Constitution didn't give women that right at first. It had to be amended, or changed. In 1920, the 19th Amendment gave women the right to vote.

Three years later, the Equal Rights Amendment (ERA) was introduced to Congress. It stated that women would be considered equal under the law. As of 2017—nearly a century later—people are still fighting to pass the ERA.

### Facing the Facts

In 1848, a group of men and women met in Seneca Falls, New York, to speak out in favor of women's rights. This is known as the Seneca Falls Convention.

The right to vote is known as suffrage, so women who fought for the right to vote, such as the women shown here, were often called suffragettes.

# The Wage Gap

People who fight for gender equality in the United States today often talk about economic equality. This means men and women make the same amount of money for doing the same job. In 1963, President John F. Kennedy signed the Equal Pay Act, which stated that people couldn't be paid less just because of their gender.

Although this is the law, women still earn less money than men in the United States. On average, a woman made 83 cents for every dollar a man made in 2015. This is often because women take breaks from their **careers** to raise children.

### Facing the Facts 🔍

As of 2015, the average woman needed to work an extra 44 days a year to earn the same amount of money as the average man in the United States.

The difference between how much money men and women earn is sometimes called the gender wage gap. Many men and women are working hard to **eliminate** this gap.

13

# Women at Work

Equal pay at work is an important part of gender equality, and another important part is equality in the kind of work that's done. One area where women are looking to have a more equal presence is in STEM (science, technology, engineering, and math) careers.

As of 2016, girls did just as well as boys in math and science classes. However, women made up only 29 percent of the STEM workforce. Many **organizations** help girls who have an interest in STEM continue on that career path.

### Facing the Facts

In 2017, women led 32 of the top 500 most **profitable** companies in the United States, according to *Fortune* magazine. Although that's only 6.4 percent, it was double the number from 2016.

Computer science is one area where women hold far fewer jobs than men. Organizations such as Girls Who Code aim to show girls that computer science is a field anyone can work in—not just men.

# An Equal Education

Education is one of the keys to a more equal world. In the United States, boys and girls generally have the same opportunities to learn and to **participate** in afterschool activities.

In 1972, a law called Title IX, or Title Nine, was passed. This law states that any school that gets money from the **federal** government has to offer girls and women the same opportunities as boys and men. It led to greater equality in classes students could take, health care students were given, sports teams students could play on, and many other parts of student life.

## Facing the Facts 🔍

Schools that teach both boys and girls are sometimes called coeducational, or coed, schools. Oberlin College became the first coed college in the United States in 1833.

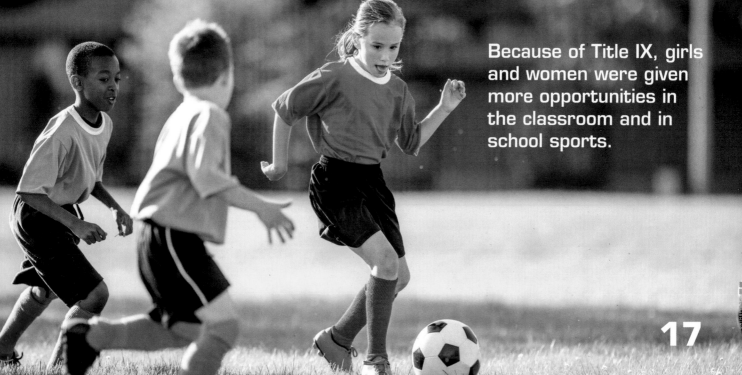

Because of Title IX, girls and women were given more opportunities in the classroom and in school sports.

17

# Women's Rights Around the World

Gender equality is an important issue around the world. It's considered a basic human right. When women have more opportunities and freedom, they make countries healthier and more economically successful. However, women and men still aren't treated as equals in many countries.

These women face **violence**, a lack of education, and an inability to make their own money or choices about their health. Groups such as the United Nations are working to make gender equality a **reality** around the world. They're giving women **access** to better health care, schools, and opportunities for work.

NEW YORK

FIRST CONVENTION FOR
WOMAN'S RIGHTS
WAS HELD ON THIS CORNER
1848

STATE EDUCATION
DEPARTMENT 1932

## Facing the Facts 🔍

Around 62 million girls worldwide aren't in school.

In 2012, Malala Yousafzai, shown here, was shot by a man in Pakistan for speaking out about the importance of educating girls. Today, she's working to make the world a more equal place by helping women and girls get an education.

# Join the Fight

People who fight for gender equality fight for a world where no one is told they can't do something because of their gender. If a boy wants to take dance classes, he should be able to. If a girl dreams of being the president, people should **encourage** her to follow that dream.

Gender equality isn't a reality yet. Men and women are still treated differently in the United States and around the world. However, there are many things people can do to make the world a more equal place for everyone. It's never too early to start doing your part!

### Facing the Facts

On January 21, 2017, more than 5 million people around the world marched for women's rights and gender equality.

# WHAT CAN YOU DO?

Respect everyone no matter what their gender is.

Raise money for groups that fight for gender equality around the world.

Read more about women's rights movements around the world.

Include both girls and boys in groups or teams at school.

Try an activity that goes against gender stereotypes.

Speak up if you feel someone isn't being treated fairly because of their gender.

Choose television shows and movies that show women and men being treated as equals.

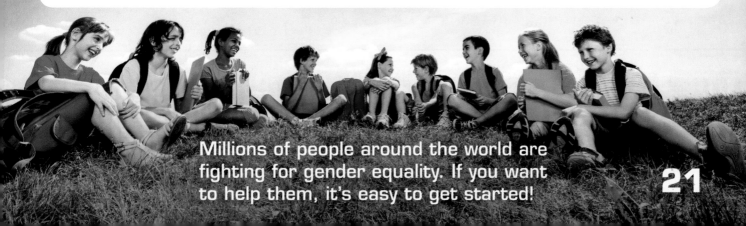

Millions of people around the world are fighting for gender equality. If you want to help them, it's easy to get started!

# GLOSSARY

**access:** The ability to use or have something.

**career:** A job a person can do for a long time.

**definition:** A statement of the meaning of a word.

**eliminate:** To put an end to or get rid of.

**encourage:** To make someone more likely to do something.

**federal:** Relating to the central government of the United States.

**organization:** A group formed for a specific purpose.

**participate:** To take part.

**profitable:** Making money.

**reality:** The way things actually are.

**treatment:** The act of treating someone or something.

**violence:** The use of bodily force to hurt others.

# FOR MORE INFORMATION

## WEBSITES

### Girlstart: STEM

*girlstart.org/tag/stem*

Girlstart is an organization that works to increase girls' interest in STEM, and this part of their website features hands-on STEM activities for both girls and boys.

### HeForShe

*www.heforshe.org*

HeForShe was started by the United Nations to encourage men and boys to learn more about gender equality issues.

## BOOKS

Clinton, Chelsea, and Alexandra Boiger. *She Persisted: 13 American Women Who Changed the World.* New York, NY: Philomel Books, 2017.

Loria, Laura. *The 19th Amendment.* New York, NY: Britannica Educational Publishing, 2017.

McAneney, Caitie. *Malala Yousafzai.* New York, NY: PowerKids Press, 2017.

# INDEX